VARNIKAA

Madhubani themed tear-out
colouring book for adults

VARNIKAA

Madhubani themed tear-out colouring book for adults

Deepika Mahalakshmi

Notion Press

Old No. 38, New No. 6
McNichols Road, Chetpet
Chennai - 600 031

First Published by Notion Press 2016
Copyright © Deepika Mahalakshmi 2016
All Rights Reserved.

ISBN 978-81-7511-095-3

Acknowledgements

I would like to express my gratitude to my family who saw me through this book, my friends Sandhiya and Rohini for supporting me right from the beginning and Eden's Edge for reproducing my designs digitally. I would like to thank my publisher - Notion press team.

To Harish my pillar of strength, best critic for his constant motivation!!

Prologue

This book is specially created to de-stress and lets you decorate your personal space with your artwork. The intricate madhubani patterns trains your brain to focus and impart the same benefits as meditation. This new hobby increases your self-esteem, reduce anxiety and calms down the mind. The beautiful patterns radiate happiness to individuals with OCD, depression, anxiety disorders.

Unleash the inner child and fill the pages with your imagination.

The art works can be coloured using pastels, pencils, pens, water colours, acrylic colours.

"The secret of getting ahead is getting started."

1. Hathor – Egyptian Sky Goddess of Love

In one famous myth and legend the Sun god Ra ruled the world but the humans turned against him and undermined his authority and had to be punished. The right "Eye of Ra," representing the sun, was depicted as his daughter Hathor, who passed judgement and many humans were killed when she turned into Sekhmet, the lioness goddess. Ra worried that she would wipe out the entire human race, so he had red dye mixed with other liquids and spread about the land. Hathor, thinking it was blood, drank it and became so intoxicated that she forgot her mission and humankind was saved until judged at the end of their lives in the Underworld. Pacified by the liquid, the goddess resumed her personality as the beautiful Hathor.

Share your thoughts

_____

_____

_____

_____

_____

_____

_____

_____

_____

_____

2. The Madhubani Fish

when life gets you down wanna know what you've got to do???

Just keep swimming!!! Just keep swimming!!!!

Share your thoughts

_____

_____

_____

_____

_____

_____

_____

_____

_____

_____

_____

_____

_____

_____

3. The Sri Yantra

If you are always trying to be normal you will never know how amazing you can be!!

Share your thoughts

_____

_____

_____

_____

_____

_____

_____

_____

_____

_____

_____

_____

_____

_____

_____

_____

_____

_____

4. The Madhubani Peacock

Be like the bird that, passing on her flight awhile on boughs too slight, Feels them give way beneath her, and yet sings, knowing that she hath wings!!

Share your thoughts

_____

_____

_____

_____

_____

_____

_____

_____

_____

_____

_____

_____

_____

_____

_____

_____

_____

5. Sunflower Mandala Garden

Let us dance in the sun wearing wild flowers in our hair!!

Share your thoughts

_____

_____

_____

_____

_____

_____

_____

_____

_____

_____

_____

_____

_____

_____

_____

_____

6. The Mirror Image

The free flowing mirror images of the flowers just like the flowing houghts that reflect the mind!!

Share your thoughts

_____

_____

_____

_____

_____

_____

_____

_____

_____

_____

_____

_____

_____

_____

_____

_____

7. Swirls and Petals

To be yourself in a world that is constantly trying to make you something else is a greatest accomplishment!!!

Share your thoughts

_____

_____

_____

_____

_____

_____

_____

_____

_____

_____

_____

_____

_____

_____

_____

_____

8. The Beloved Ganesha

Varâha-Purâna, Ganesh is depicted like a wonderfully handsome young man originating from the glittering forehead of Shiva absorbed in a deep meditation. This mânasika putra, son-born-from the Shiva's mind, was a dazzling human boy. Pârvatî was disappointed that the boy was born without her intervention. So, she wished that his head became the head of an elephant. However, when she saw the elephant-headed child, she loved him immediately, and declared that any human or divine undertaking, should not be successful unless Ganesh/Ganapati would be worshipped first.

Share your thoughts

_____

_____

_____

_____

_____

_____

_____

_____

_____

_____

_____

9. The Spring Fish

Inspired by the Anemone fishes that live in groups where the two largest fish only are the mature ones , the largest being female and the next largest male. If the female dies, the male changes to female and the next largest fish in the group matures to male. If the animated film "Finding Nemo," had been true to life, Nemo's dad, Marlin, should have become Nemo's mother shortly after his original mother was eaten by a barracuda.

Share your thoughts

_____

_____

_____

_____

_____

_____

_____

_____

_____

_____

_____

_____

10. The Spirited Woman

A woman in harmony with het spirit is like a river flowing. She goes where she will without pretense and arrives at her destination prepared to be herself and only herself.

Share your thoughts

_____

_____

_____

_____

_____

_____

_____

_____

_____

_____

_____

_____

_____

_____

_____

_____

11. The Peacock Fish

Try to be a rainbow in someone's cloud!!

Share your thoughts

_____

_____

_____

_____

_____

_____

_____

_____

_____

_____

_____

_____

_____

_____

_____

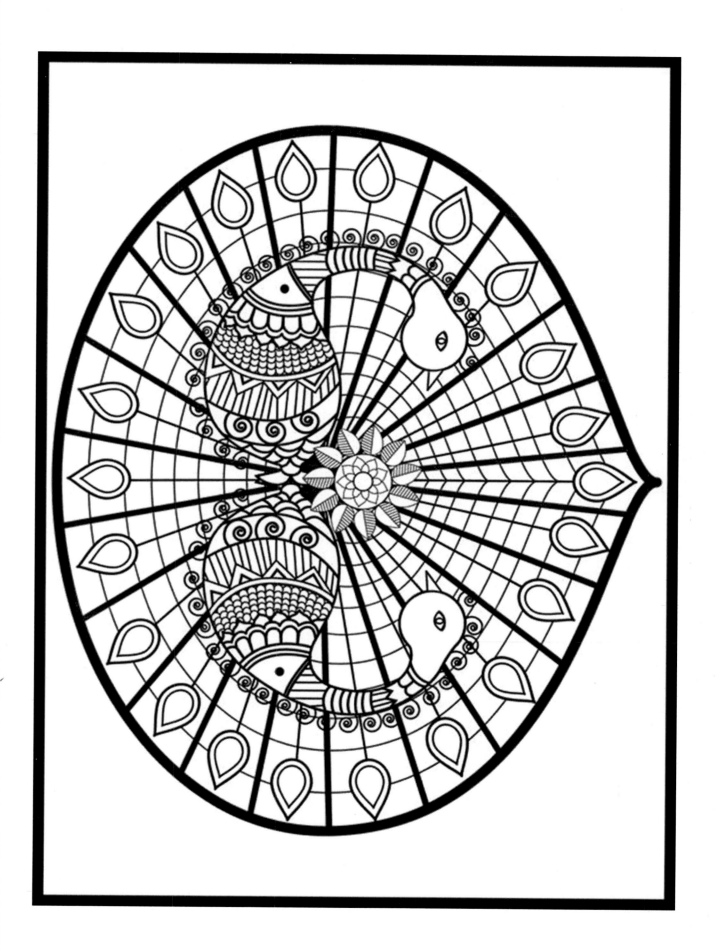

12. The Madhubani Sun God - Surya

Surya, the sun god radiates the energy of life in a madhubani painting. Surya symbolises power and hope!!

Share your thoughts

_____

_____

_____

_____

_____

_____

_____

_____

_____

_____

_____

_____

_____

_____

_____

13. Surya Vahini – The Madhubani Female Sun God!!

Turn your face towards the sun and the shadows fall behind you. Smile like the bright sun that you are.

Share your thoughts

_____

_____

_____

_____

_____

_____

_____

_____

_____

_____

_____

_____

_____

_____

_____

14. The Traditional Hindu Floor Art – Kolam

Imagination will often carry us to worlds that never wer, but without it we go nowhere!!

Share your thoughts

_____

_____

_____

_____

_____

_____

_____

_____

_____

_____

_____

_____

_____

_____

_____

_____

15. Thoth – Egyptian God of Wealth and Wisdom

According to one myth Horus lost his left eye in his war with Set who tore the eye into six pieces. Thoth, the god of wisdom and magic, was able to reassemble the eye and return it to Horus who gave the reassembled eye to his murdered father Osiris, thereby bringing him back to life. He is associated with jackal-headed god Anubis at the 'Weighing of the Heart' and with the Seshat, his female counterpart and the goddess of writing and libraries. Thoth also plays an important role in the legend concerning the Tree of Life.

Share your thoughts

_____

_____

_____

_____

_____

_____

_____

_____

_____

_____

_____

16. The Mandala Sun

Laughter is timeless, imagination has no age, dreams are forever!!!

Share your thoughts

_____

_____

_____

_____

_____

_____

_____

_____

_____

_____

_____

_____

_____

_____

_____

_____

17. The Autumn Flowers

Flutter your wings

as if your branches were swaying

spread your feathers

like your blooming flowers

You are the beauty

of a hummingbird

and stand still

of a cherry blossom

Share your thoughts

_____

_____

_____

_____

_____

_____

_____

_____

_____

_____

18. Queen Ahmose Nefertari

The queen was revered as "Goddess of Resurrection" and was arguably the most venerated women in Egyptian history reference to her position as the mother of Egypt. She generally wears the vulture headdress of Nekhbet. She was the first queen to hold the important office of "God's Wife of Amun." 'Lady of the West' and 'Mistress of the Sky.'

Share your thoughts

_____

_____

_____

_____

_____

_____

_____

_____

_____

_____

_____

_____

_____

19. The Poo Kolam

Colour away your imagination!!!!

Share your thoughts

_____

_____

_____

_____

_____

_____

_____

_____

_____

_____

_____

_____

_____

_____

_____

_____

_____

20. Sobek

According to some ancient Egyptian myths Sobek was the son of Neith and Set. His consort was Renenutet, the snake goddess who was the protector of the harvest and granaries. Sobek began as a deity of fertility and water. Then myths associated him with creation and the River Nile was believed to have come from the sweat of Sobek and gave life to vegetation and was credited with the fertility of the land. One of his titles was 'Lord of the Waters' as Sobek.

Share your thoughts

_____

_____

_____

_____

_____

_____

_____

_____

_____

_____

_____

_____